YOUR KNOWLEDGE HAS VALUE

Haider Madhloum

African American Vernacular English - Origins and Features

GRIN Publishing

Bibliographic information published by the German National Library:

The German National Library lists this publication in the National Bibliography;
detailed bibliographic data are available on the Internet at http://dnb.dnb.de .

Imprint:

Copyright © 2011 GRIN Verlag, Open Publishing GmbH
Print and binding: Books on Demand GmbH, Norderstedt Germany
ISBN: 978-3-640-85605-3

This book at GRIN:

http://www.grin.com/en/e-book/168294/african-american-vernacular-english-origins-
and-features

GRIN - Your knowledge has value

Since its foundation in 1998, GRIN has specialized in publishing academic texts by students, college teachers and other academics as e-book and printed book. The website www.grin.com is an ideal platform for presenting term papers, final papers, scientific essays, dissertations and specialist books.

Visit us on the internet:

http://www.grin.com/

http://www.facebook.com/grincom

http://www.twitter.com/grin_com

Haider MADHLOUM

TKO MECHELEN

AFRICAN AMERICAN Vernacular English

ASO
Engels MTAL 4

Schooljaar 2010-2011
1ste Trimester

Table of contents

1. Introduction_____ 4
2. What is AAVE?_____ 5
    2.1. Who speaks AAVE?_____ 6
3. The origins of AAVE_____ 7
    3.1. The Afrocentric view_____ 7
    3.2. The Eurocentric view_____ 7
    3.3. The Creolist view_____ 8
4. The Oakland school Board proposal_____ 9
5. Features of AAVE_____ 10
    5.1. Phonological features_____ 10
    5.2. Grammatical features_____ 12
        5.2.1. Tense and aspect_____ 12
            5.2.1.1.   Optional past-tense marking_____ 12
            5.2.1.2.   Obligatory aspect marking_____ 12
            5.2.1.3.   Markers of tense, mood and aspect_____ 13
            5.2.1.4.   Semantic features_____ 15
            5.2.1.5.   Negation_____ 15
    5.3. Lexicon of AAVE_____ 16
6. Conclusion_____ 18
7. List of references_____ 19

Acknowledgments

I would like to thank all the people who helped me to make this paper. The list includes TKO student Zoulikha El Bouchtati, who printed this paper for me. This paper was completed during my 3rd semester on TKO Mechelen, and I am especially thankful to the excellent facilities of the school and their efficient, supportive staff: Liesbeth Piessens and Vera Lapeere and the other staff members at TKO Mechelen.

1. Introduction

African American Vernacular English (AAVE) is the variety formerly known as Black English Vernacular or Vernacular Black English among sociolinguists. It is also called Ebonics outside the academic community. While some features of AAVE are apparently unique to this variety, in its structure it also shows many similarities with other varieties including a number of standard and nonstandard English varieties spoken in the US. AAVE has been the subject of several public debates. The analysis of this variety has caused a lot of discussion among sociolinguists and also among the American people.

AAVE is a language that I hear every day through the music I hear and the Internet I use. This was the main reason that I chose to learn more about AAVE. Many people think AAVE is the same as Standard American English but this is not true.

In this paper I will investigate whether AAVE is a dialect or a slang. And also the origins of AAVE and the features of AAVE (Phonological-, grammatical and lexical features) and the social and educational context of AAVE will be explained more in this paper.

Through many research in the library of the university of Antwerp and the library of the university of Leuven but also through many research on the internet I was able to collect and investigate this subject. With the great help of my teacher Mvr. Piessens I was able to make this paper.

2. What is AAVE?

"AAVE is a nonstandard form of American English Characteristically spoken by African Americans in the United States of America"(Miller, G. (2010) (online))
There is a difference between Ebonics and AAVE; Ebonics is the language that slaves and people who where directly imported from Africa used, this language used a lot of slang features. The difference is that Ebonics is the precursor of AAVE; AAVE arose after Ebonics and is more distinguished and is more developed than Ebonics.
AAVE gained public attention on 16 December 1996, When the Oakland (California) school board approved a resolution that would recognize AAVE as a primary language in the USA. This resolution to the school Board resolution will be explained later in this paper.

The reactions in the USA to the school Board resolution were very negative. Many sociolinguists as well as the American people were not pleased with this resolution. On the Internet many people expressed their anger against this resolution. The main reason was that many people thought that AAVE would be taught in the classroom. But this was not true. The school board's plan was to have special programs for teachers to get to know AAVE better, so they could help African American students with learning Standard American English. These students had a lot of problems because of the differences between Standard American English and AAVE. You could conclude that the idea of the Oakland school Board was to use the vernacular[1] to teach the Standard.

When we read that Linguists have approved a proposal and that they support this proposal, we should ask what the main task is of a linguist?
A linguist is someone who studies the sounds, words and grammar of languages and dialects. The following three principles of the goal of linguists will make you understand more why they approved this proposition.
"The first principle of the science of linguists is that linguists need to describe how people talk". This means that they don't have the right to judge a language on how it needs to be used, they only need to describe it. "the second principle is that all languages, if they have enough speakers, have dialects". And the last principle is that 'all languages and dialects are systematic and rule-governed".

Now , knowing these principles we can understand why many linguists describe AAVE as a dialect and not as a slang. The main definition of a dialect is "A regional or social variety of a language distinguished by pronunciation, grammar, or vocabulary, especially a variety of speech differing from the standard literary language or speech pattern of the culture in which it exists" (Houghton Mifflin Company. (2009) The American heritage; dictionary of the English language,[online] Available: http://www.thefreedictionary.com/dialect [17 Dec 2010])
AAVE can be identified by the definition of a dialect.

Linguists (not all linguists) were pleased by the resolution of The Oakland School Board. At the annual meeting of Linguistic Society of America, a resolution was approved describing AAVE as "systematic and rule-governed like all natural speech varieties". They also agreed that the proposition was "linguistically and pedagogically sound".

---

[1] Vernacular means a language that people speak that is not an official language. It the tongue that people use to express their selves.

We can conclude that AAVE is not a slang but a dialect, even if we see that AAVE has some slang words such as *chillin* ("relaxing") and *homey* ("close friend").
The manner in which AAVE differs from Standard English is highly ordered: this means that AAVE has a grammatical structure, specific word usage and a phonology that is distinguished. If we analyze AAVE we will understand the complex rules that African American speakers follow effortlessly and unconsciously in their daily lives. (Rickford, 1999: 320-322)

2.1. Who speaks AAVE?

Nobody uses all the rules of AAVE at once (grammar and pronunciation), most people who speak AAVE use a sort of mixture of AAVE and Standard American English.

Most speakers are African Americans, however not all African Americans speak AAVE. Here we make a distinction between AAVE and Ebonics. Ebonics is the Old English spoken during the 1800's and 1900's, it is the language that slaves spoke. There were many slang words in this slang used. AAVE is a dialect that is mostly spoken by African Americans, it is a developed dialect with many rules on the grammatical- phonological and lexical parts.

Most speakers of the African American community are among the working-class. This due to the fact that people still see AAVE as a language that is not very appropriate to use in higher classes. It is more a street language, that is why it is mostly spoken among adolescents. It is much used in the informal contexts (e.g. a conversation on the streets). In the writing language many use Standard American English, this is more accepted by the community, because SAE has a more formal status.

Social networks also influence who speaks AAVE. Higher class people such as doctors and lawyers speak Standard American English (in social environment) more than laborers and the unemployed.

The sense of community is an explanation for the evolution of AAVE. Many African Americans did not belong to the community of the white people (they did not have contact with white people) and were driven into ghettos. They used AAVE to create a community. That is why many working-class speakers (and adolescents) use AAVE. Because AAVE would identify them with a community in which they lived, namely the African American community.

Some slang features of AAVE were used in other varieties of English especially the Southern White dialects. Many slaves worked in southern America, There was a heavy concentration of African Americans (slaves). But these features were slang because it was the early development of the AAVE language. Expressions like "givin five" and "whassup?" were (and are now) so much used in the American culture that many people don't realize they originated in the African American community (Rickford, 1999: 323-324).

We could conclude that AAVE was the language of the working-class people (who were African Americans). The social network also influenced the usage of this dialect and that AAVE speakers spoke AAVE to create a sense of community in the ghettos.

3. The origins of AAVE

The first Africans were 'imported' to the United States as slaves from 1619 to 1808, they arrived in Jamestown.
These people all spoke other languages because they came from another continent namely Western Africa. After they arrived, they tried to learn the English language, but because there was no contact between the black slaves and white people they didn't learn the language optimally. So they learned the language with much influence of their own native language. But how much did their native language influence the learning of this new language? Many linguists do not agree on the origins of AAVE. There are mainly 3 views on the origins of AAVE. Which are those views?

3.1. The Afrocentric view

The first view is the Afrocentric view. This view says that most distinctive features are imported from Africa. This means that the features that AAVE uses originated from Africa. The slaves converted the English language to the patterns of the Niger-Congo languages.

There is however, not one particular West-African language which is the base of AAVE. Afrocentrics can not prove that all of the distinctive features of AAVE originated from Western Africa. In AAVE final consonants are dropped (e.g. "five" →*fi*), a feature that is found in England dialects, but English dialects have nothing to do with West-African language. West-African /Niger Congo language do not drop final consonants.(Rickford, 1999:324-327)

3.2. The Eurocentric view

A second view is the Eurocentic view. Dialectologists are supporters of this view. They justify their view by the following argument : "African slaves learned English from white settlers, and they did so relatively fast and successfully, retaining little trace of their African linguistic heritage"(Rickford, 1999: 325-326).

Eurocentrics also think that Urban ghettos (in the 20th century) were a base for the AAVE features.

Here we have the same problem as with the Afrocentric arguments: basic and crucial features of AAVE, such as the absence of the linking-verb "is", do not exist in the early settler dialects. So these could not have been the source.

However, there are two theories that could support this view:

1. "African American slaves and whites sometimes worked alongside each other in households and fields". This means that African Americans could have picked up the English language here.

2. "The number of African slaves was so low (especially in the early colonial period) that AAVE may not have been formed". This means that African Americans could picked up the English language (as a base for AAVE) here.

We can not assume that the slaves learned the dialects of the whites around them because this requires more evidence of their relationship (Rickford, 1999: 325-326).

3.3. The Creolist view

A third view is the Creolist view. This means that many African slaves (with the help of English) created a pidgin language[2]. This language is created (by its speakers) to make it easier to communicate with each other when both people do not speak the same language. It becomes a Creole language when it becomes established and also becomes the primary tongue among its users.
This was the fact among children of Pidgin speakers.

Creole languages are spoken on the islands of the Caribbean and the Pacific, because there were large plantations where many slaves worked. On these fields new languages were created e.g. Haitian Creole French and Jamaican Creole English. This was due to the fact that many slaves (from different backgrounds, but in general blacks and whites) had to work together and there was no contact between the slaves and the white settlers.
In the United States African Americans speak mainly one English Creole, Gullah. This language is spoken on the Sea-Islands off the coast of South Carolina and Georgia. In these two places the local population consists of 70% African Americans.

The Creole speech was introduced to the United States because many slaves were imported from the colonies in Jamaica and Barbados. In these places 70% of the habitants were Africans.

There were also slaves who were directly imported from Africa, they might have brought pidgins with them.

And some pidgins might have developed in America. This was mainly in Southern-America, where many Africans were imported to work as slaves on the land. (Rickford, 1999: 326-327)

---

[2] " A mixed language incorporating elements of its users' native language but with less complex grammar and fewer words than either parent language" Rickford R. , J. (1999) *African American Vernacular English*, Massachusetts: Blackwell Publishers Inc.

4. The Oakland School Board Proposal

The Oakland School Board (California) Proposal was a proposal to recognize AAVE. The Oakland School Board passed a resolution that would recognize AAVE as a language. This resolution set off a lot of media criticism and was the cause for a national debate.

The resolution meant that for students whose primary dialect was AAVE, from now on AAVE would be recognized as a language. This meant that there would be rules in how to teach this language in both grammar as lexicon.
This would develop "maintaining the legitimacy and richness of such language and to facilitate their acquisition and mastery of English language skills".
(Wikipedia (2010) Oaklands Ebonics controversy [online], available: http://en.wikipedia.org /wiki/Oakland_Ebonics_controversy [9 Dec 2010])

The reason why there was so much criticism were under the wrong impression that schools would be teaching AAVE to their students. However, the Oakland School Board said: "that the intent was not to teach AAVE as a distinct language but to use it as a tool to increase mastery of Standard English among AAVE speakers. The support of linguists for this approach may strike nonlinguists as unorthodox, but that is where our principles leads us".

Using features of AAVE to learn Standard English has many advantages. In this way the teachers would be able to teach students Standard American English by using AAVE (Using the Vernacular to teach the Standard). This would be an advantage Experiments have showed that when teachers use the vernacular to teach the Standard language students learn Standard American English faster.

The following experiment was taken at Aurora University, outside Chicago. The teachers at this university used a method that contrasted Standard English and AAVE features through explicit instructions and drills. This duration of this test was 11 weeks. After these 11 weeks the students showed a 59% reduction of the use of AAVE, when they were asked to make a test on Standard English writing.

The method I explained in the example above was promoted by the Oakland School Board. They needed this method because in the past teachers failed to teach African American students who spoke AAVE (at home or on the street) the Standard American English language (Rickford, 1999: 327-328).

5. Features of AAVE

5.1. Phonological features

Phonology is "the study of the sound system of a given language and the analysis and classification of its phonemes"(Miller (2009)).

In the late 1960s and early 1970s there were many difficulties in teaching young African Americans Standard English. Linguists saw the phonological differences between AAVE and Standard American English crucial to the reading difficulties and standardized test biases[3] faced by African American children. If linguists and teachers were able to recognize these 'problems', they would be able to teach the children Standard American English more easily and in a correct way.

First, I explain what the phonological features of AAVE are. There are a lot of features, but in this paper I will explain 12 features typical of AAVE. These are the most important differences between SAE and AAVE.

1- Loss of the 2nd consonant in AAVE, at the end of a word the consonant is not pronounced . This phenomenon also appears in other varieties of English, but it is most frequent in AAVE.
   For example: "cold" → *col_* and "hand" → *han_*

2- Deletion of one unstressed syllable of a word. This is also called "unstressed syllable deletion". This is most frequent in AAVE, but it is also found in other English varieties.
   For example: "about" → *_bout* and "government" → *gov'ment*

3- Hapology (the deletion of a reduplicated syllable). This means that a syllable which is written double in a word is not pronounced. This is common in most English varieties.
   For example: "Mississippi" → *Misipi* and "general" → *genral*

4- Vocalization of postvocalic /l/.
   For example: "Bell" → *Bell* (there is producing of sound at the end-l)

5- Loss of /r/ after consonants . This is common in other non-standard varieties, especially in southern America. It means that the /r/ is not pronounced when it follows on a consonant.
   For example: "throw" → *thou* and "professor" → *pofesse* → you write the r down but you don't pronounce it.

6- Replacing interdential fricatives by f.
   For example: "bath" → *baf* and "baths" → *bafs*

7- Syllable-initial fricative stopping.
   For example: "those" → *dose* and "these" → *deze*

8- Stopping of voiceless interdental fricatives:
   For example: "Tenth" → *tent* and "with" → *wit*

---

[3] Systematical faults.

9- Reduction of final nasal to vowel nasality. This is unique to AAVE.
  For example: "man" →*mae*

10- Deletion of the final consonant, the final consonant isn't pronounced. This is unique to AAVE.
  For example: "five" →*fi_* and "fine" →*fi_*

11- Loss of /j/ after consonants. This is unique to AAVE.
  For example: "computer" → *compure* and "Houston" → *hustn.*

12- Substitution of /k/ for /t/ in /str/ clusters. This is apparently unique to AAVE.
  For example: "street" → *skrit* and "stream" →*skrim*

  (Mufwene, Rickford, Bailey, Baugh, 1998: 85-90)

Phonology is important in AAVE, because phonological features are often used to teach children the Standard, to help them with, for example, speech therapy. Phonological features are often the base for language discrimination by its listeners. The phonology of AAVE shows that African Americans have problems with learning the SAE language and that they need help to solve these problems with e.g. speech therapy. The features showed in the above examples makes phonology an ideal base for future research on AAVE. (Mufwene, Rickford, Bailey, Baugh 1998: 107)

Verb stems
There are many verbs who differ in AAVE in contrast to Standard American English.

Here are some examples.

The verb "fill" is used as "full" in AAVE.
This means that when the sentence is Standard American English is: "he filling the tank", in AAVE this is said: "he fullin' the tank".

The past form of the verb "leave" is used as "lef" in AAVE. This is shown by following example:
"he left town" is in AAVE "he lef town"

AAVE speakers do not use the word "ask" but they convert it into *aks*
E.g. "he asks directions" is converted into "he *aks* directions.

5.2. Grammatical features

5.2.1. Tense and aspect.

5.2.1.1. Optional past-tense Marking

In standard English the marking of verb tense is required while marking of verb aspect is optional.

In AAVE the reverse is true, marking of tense is optional and marking of verb aspect is required. An action in the past may be represented by the base form of the verb.
E.g. the SE sentence: "I fed the cat and washed the dishes and swept the floor"
Would make in AAVE: " I feed the cat and wash the dishes and sweep the floor".
This sentence in AAVE could be either past or present.
An alternative for the AAVE sentence is "I fed the cat and wash the dishes and sweep the floor". AAVE speakers can use one past tense in a sentence to indicate the past.
Another alternative to mark the past is the use of tense by non-verb lexical items such as "yesterday" and "the day before".
E.g. "Yesterday, I feed the dog and wash the dishes".

5.2.1.2. Obligatory Aspect marking

In an AAVE sentence the verb "be" is not used as a linking verb.
For example: "they are really fine" → "they real fine".

The verb "be" is used to mark aspects as habitual or continuous.
There are two sentences that will show the difference:
- "He workin' when the boss come in" -- This means that he just works when the boss comes in= habitual.
- "he be workin' when the boss come in" – This means that he's typically working when the boss comes in = continuous.
Another example that many linguists use to show a difference between verb with "be" is "you makin' sense, but you don't be makin' sense" – this means that you make sense right now, but generally you don't make sense/

5.2.1.3.   Markers of tense, mood and aspect

The following 10 aspects are the most important features of AAVE. These are most frequently used and are very specific for the AAVE language.

1. The absence of auxiliary "is" and "are" for present states and actions. This is most used in the AAVE language. When Arab and Hebrew people speak English this shows up in their language.
    To give an example: 'he is tall" is in AAVE: "he tall"

2. The use of invariant "be" (sometimes it is also used as "bees") for habitual aspects. This is unique to the AAVE language, and is one of the most specific feature of this language.
    E.g. "He is walking" → "he be walking" in AAVE.

3. The use of "steady" as an intensified continuative marker. Not frequently used in AAVE, but is a big difference between Standard American English and AAVE.
    E.g. "Haider Madhloum be steady steppin' in them number nines".

4. The use of invariant "be" for future. This means that when AAVE speakers refer to the future of an action they always use the verb "be".
    E.g. in Standard American English: "He will be here tomorrow" becomes in AAVE: "He be here tomorrow".

5. The use of unstressed "been" and "BIN" for has/have.
    E.g. "He has been sick" in AAVE: "he been sick".

6. The use of stressed "BIN" to mark that the Action happened or that the state came into being long ago.
    E.g. In SAE: "she has been married for a long time" becomes in AAVE: "She bin married".

7. The use of "done" to point up the completed nature of an action. "Done" is used to mark that the action is completed.
    E.g. in SAE: "He's already done it" becomes in AAVE: " he done did it".

8. The use of *finna* to mark the immediate future. This means that when some person is going to to do something in the direct future AAVE speakers replace the sentence verbs "to be about to" by *finna*
    E.g. In SAE : He's about to go" becomes in AAVE: "he *finna* go".

9. The use of "come" to express the speakers outrage (emotion) about an action or event. When the AAVE speaker uses "come" this is used in a way that the speaker uses it to emphasize his emotion about an action. E.g. In AAVE: "he *come* walkin' in here like he owned the place" This means that the speaker is outraged about the way he comes walked in. This is a reaction by the speaker on an action of the person who comes in the room.

10. The use of "had" to mark the simple past.
E.g. In SAE: "the we went outside" becomes in AAVE: "then we has went outside".

11. The use of double modals in tenses. (modals such as *may can, might can and might could.*)
E.g. in SAE: he *might* be able to" becomes in AAVE: "He *might can* be able to".

12. The replacement of the SAE tense aspect "must not" to *must don't* in AAVE.

13. As you may have noticed in some sentences that I have used in this paper (especially in the tense part) that verbs ending on –*ing* aren't written in AAVE.
E.g. "waiting" in SAE becomes *waitin'* in AAVE.
Or "speaking" in SAE becomes *speakin'* in AAVE.

Some of these 13 previous most important features of tense marking in AAVE are also used by other speakers of American English. These are mostly two groups of people namely Arab people and Hebrew people. Also fellow Americans use these features when they put a post on their Facebook or Twitter account (the new internet posts). (Google (2010))

5.2.1.4.   Semantic features

Semantics means the study of word meanings in a language.

Words with two or more meanings.
 Mostly these words are each others contrary.
To give an example of contrary meanings of a word in AAVE.
"he is a *bad* man"
In this sentence the word "bad" has two meanings.
The positive meaning of this word is that it means that the man is "a person of highly desirable character". The negative meaning of this word is "a person of undesirable character".
There are other words like "bad" namely: *nigger, cool and clean.*

Words with two-levelled meanings
"You look *cool*, mam"
In this sentence the word *cool* has meanings on two levels this is also called "counterlanguage" in the linguistic jargon. This typical AAVE feature can only be understood by insiders.
It could mean that "her outer appearance is not dirty, as usual" or that "she is wearing an elegant dress".

Morpho-syntax: This means that a word in AAVE can be used as a noun and also as a verb.
E.g.
The word *pimp* can be a
Noun: " a man who lives frome the earnings of a prostitute".
Verb: "to dress and walk like a pimp" or "to exploit someone".

5.2.1.5.   Negation

The part of negations (in the grammatical part) is a very important part due to its frequent use in the AAVE language.

There are 3 major differences in the AAVE language

1- The use of *ain'(t)* as "am not", "isn't", "aren't", "hasn't", haven't", "didn't".
   E.g. In SAE: "he *isn't* on school" becomes in AAVE: "he *ain't* on school".

2- The use of multiple negation by AAVE speakers.
   E.g. in SAE: "He *doesn't* do *anything*" becomes in AAVE: "he *don't* do *nothing*".

3- The use of *ain't but* and *don't but* to replace the SAE word "only".
E.g. In SAE: " He's only fourteen years old" becomes in AAVE: "he *ain't but* fourteen years old".

5.3. Lexicon of AAVE

The AAVE lexicon means "the dynamic, colorful span of language used by African Americans from all walks of life" (Mufwene, S., Rickford, J., Bailey, G., Baugh, J. (1998): 201)

The 1960s *Black freedom Struggle*[4] was a sort of beginning of the so-called Hip Hop fashion of wearing caps with a large "X" (Malcolm X) written on it, they're called *X caps* in AAVE lexicon. Black people wanted to show the world that they have a culture and an own language just to be recognized in the American community, not just as people who couldn't read nor write or who had no rights.

Many Lexicon also derived from basketball players from the *old school* times (1960s-1970s). In these areas (mostly they are in a centred place in the ghetto) many Black Africans gathered to play *alley ball* (basketball). This was a place where many African Americans socialized between each other. From These places words like *trash talkin'* derived. *Trash talkin'* means that opponents in the basketball game talk negative about each other in order to unnerve the opponent.
This early language was mostly slang.

AAVE gained many attention when television programs like "MTV" (music television) and "Def Jam Comedy" aired. These 2 channels (broadcasted on American TV) where very popular in the 1980s. Black artists like Dr. Dre and Snoop Dogg who made many Hits during these days (1982-1983) used AAVE in their raps. Rap songs where very popular in the 1980s because Black people used raps (just like their ancestors used Blues) to express their anger against the social state in America. People watched "MTV" in the whole world and there are many people who used language they heard in Raps, songs of Black artists on "MTV". What many people didn't knew was that that language was AAVE and not SAE. Words like *nigga* and *bitch* and words with *–ass* (*ass* has several meanings in AAVE just as in the previous chapter grammar was explained, e.g. I saw his *ass* yesterday – (SAE) I saw *him* yesterday) where (are still) widely known by many people and were known as SAE.

There is one specific word that is until now anno. 2010 heavily discussed namely *nigga*. Nigger (SAE) was the name given to the people who were 'imported' as slaves

---

[4] "The term *Black freedom struggle* characterizes the mass organized movement for Black empowerment that began with Mrs. Rosa Parks' now famous refusal to surrender her bus seat to a white man in Montgomery, Alabama, on 1 December 1955" (Mufwene, S., Rickford, J., Bailey, G., Baugh, J. (1998): 204)

from Africa into America. That's why it has a very negative meaning. Many Black Americans become very angry when people use that word to address Black Americans. The big discussion is "who can and who can't say the word nigger (or in AAVE *nigga)*" Among African Americans (mostly people under the age of 30 – youth) the word *nigga* has a meaning like in SAE "guy" or "man". It's used to address each other on e.g. the Basketball court. But if African Americans use it why can't White people use it, and who (of the Whites) is allowed to say it. Well, this question rises a lot of confusion among white people.

There are some situation where it is allowed for a White person to address a Black person as *nigga*. Whites who are friends with Black people and when it is not used as a word of cultural dominance (against the Black people) it is allowed to say the N. word. For example: On a basketball court or in a rap battle. In other situations it is not allowed! (Mufwene, Rickford, Bailey, Baugh 1998: 204-241)

6. Conclusion

AAVE today is a dialect which is recognized by most linguists in America. There may be discussion between linguists but facts and also features of AAVE show that AAVE is a dialect and not a slang. If the Ancestors of the modern African Americans would know that their slang is now a dialect, they would be very proud. It is a dialect that is known all over the world and is one of the most spoken dialects all over the world. People know AAVE mostly from music videos they see on various music channels (e.g. "MTV").

Most African Americans see this language as a distinguishing of their own culture. This is why they attach so much attention to it.

Nowadays teachers use AAVE to help children with an African American background to learn Standard American English. They use the vernacular to teach the standard. This is a method that is highly recommended by many linguists. This method is achieving its goal namely to help African American youth to learn the Standard American English better.

This method , responsive to the linguistic needs of every student, will prove to be one of the ultimate tests of systemic reform. The discussion between linguistics is provided in support of that effort, because greater linguistic awareness of students, along with greater tolerance for linguistic diversity, will be essential to the future educational welfare of all students, from all backgrounds.

7. List of references

Books:

Salikoko, S.M. (1998) *African-American English structure, history, and use*, London: Routledge.

Rickford R. , J. (1999) *African American Vernacular English*, Massachusetts: Blackwell Publishers Inc.

Baugh, J. (2000) *Beyond Ebonics: Linguistic pride and racial prejudice*, New York: Oxford university press.

Websites:

Miller, G. (2010) *AAVE*, [online], available:
http://wordnetweb.princeton.edu/perl/webwn?s=AAVE&sub=Search+WordNet&o2=&o0=1&o7=&o5=&o1=1&o6=&o4=&o3=&h= [17 Dec 2010]

Houghton Mifflin Company. (2009) The American heritage; dictionary of the English language,[online] Available: http://www.thefreedictionary.com/dialect [17 Dec 2010]

Wikipedia (2010), *Indentured servant* [online] available :
http://en.wikipedia.org/wiki/Indentured_servant [2 Dec 2010]

Wikipedia (2010) Oaklands Ebonics controversy [online], available:
http://en.wikipedia.org /wiki/Oakland_Ebonics_controversy [9 Dec 2010]

Miller A., G. (2009) *Phonology*, [online], available:
http://wordnetweb.princeton.edu/perl/webwn?s=phonology [17 Dec 2010]

Google (2010) *semantic aspects of AAVE* [online], available:
http://docs.google.com/viewer?a=v&q=cache:EZ8bOb7142kJ:www.uni-giessen.de/anglistik/ling/Staff/huber/HOsEnglishDialects/HO%2520Holder.doc+tense+AAVE&hl=nl&gl=be&pid=bl&srcid=ADGEEShTjWX8qzkrSAY6blCSsP32ky2Q_FXQaXWzC_mW4AXaFjbWSEu6K3Vkqx5N9qDZk-ftcKqzqGtNmG1CoHNCqLO28RmePxQkuLjOT0wpAg_d7Su_74q_evt2sS1pmsmL2Hgj78Bj&sig=AHIEtbQCkTETTCKaYN7eRZ9zv6rc8Lrq3Q [20 Dec 2010]